Paleontologist to Archaeologist
What do they do? Archaeology for Kids

Children's Biological Science of Fossils Books

BOBO's
LITTLE BRIANIAC BOOKS

educational & informative books for children
(PRE-K / K-12)

Who unearthed those precious dinosaur bones? Who told us about them?

Read on to learn and compare the responsibilities of a paleontologist and an archaeologist.

Palaeontology and archaeology may have similar aspects but they have different goals.

These two fields in Science may work together but are quite different from each other.

Palaeontology Paleontology is linked to geology. It is a branch of Science that studies fossils. It is a complex field of study.

Paleontologists unearth and study fossils. Through their work, we learn what Earth was like billions of years ago.

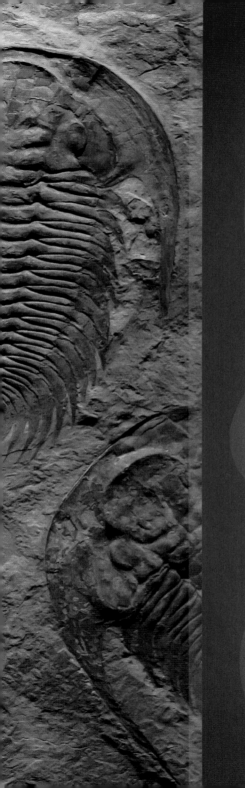

The fossils they find tell us our planet's story. Through them, we learn about evolution and ecology.

Fossils are not the whole organisms. Rather, they are tracks and imprints left in sedimentary rocks.

Through them, we learn how the organisms looked like and when they lived.

This is pretty amazing.
Being a complex field
of scientific study,
paleontology is divided
into sub-disciplines:

The paleobotonists (study plant fossils) and the micropaleontologists (study microscopic fossils).

Paleontologists also collect natural resources. These natural resources, like oil and coal, are buried underground.

In order to find them, paleontologists study the rocks and minerals where these natural resources are found

A paleontologist studies fossils. He does not just dig up

What is Archaeology?

What do archaeologists do?

Archaeology is the study of human remains and artifacts.

Archaeologist study artifacts and these are a lot like fossils!

But unlike paleontologist, archaeologists focus on human remains and history.

Just like the paleontologists, archaeologists put together the pieces of ancient evidences to prove something about how humans lived.

What are human artifacts?

These refer to things made, used and left by humans.

Examples of artifacts are hunting weapons and eating tools.

Artifacts tell us about past human civilizations. Archaeologists recreate the stories of people and cultures from the past through artifacts.

The historical information they gather will allow us to realize and appreciate our shared heritage.

To summarize, a paleontologist digs up bones of organisms while an archaeologist digs up human cultural artifacts.

Both of them excavate to learn about the past and help us better understand the present.

Would you like to be a paleontologist or an archaeologist someday?

Made in the USA
Coppell, TX
01 December 2023

25091430R00026